10/17
973, 8 Ham

1050

CIVIL WAR AFTERMATH AND RECONSTRUCTION

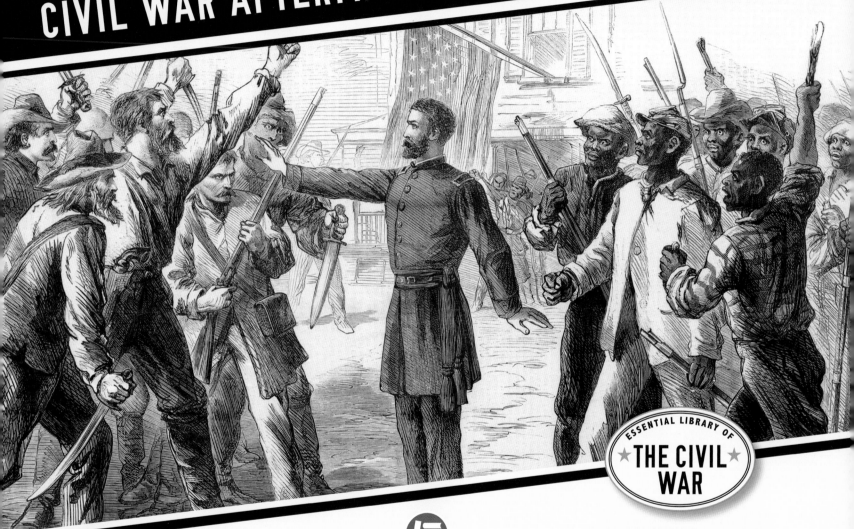

Essential Library

An Imprint of Abdo Publishing
abdopublishing.com

ESSENTIAL LIBRARY OF
★ THE CIVIL WAR ★

BY SUSAN E. HAMEN

CONTENT CONSULTANT

MARK ELLIOTT, PHD
UNIVERSITY OF NORTH CAROLINA
AT GREENSBORO

abdopublishing.com

Published by Abdo Publishing, a division of ABDO, PO Box 398166, Minneapolis, Minnesota 55439. Copyright © 2017 by Abdo Consulting Group, Inc. International copyrights reserved in all countries. No part of this book may be reproduced in any form without written permission from the publisher. Essential Library™ is a trademark and logo of Abdo Publishing.

Printed in the United States of America, North Mankato, Minnesota

052016
092016

Cover Photo: Everett Historical/Shutterstock Images
Interior Photos: Everett Historical/Shutterstock Images, 1; AS400 DB/Corbis, 4, 50, 52, 72; Library of Congress, 7, 9, 12, 23, 24, 35, 36, 38, 47, 49, 55, 56, 61, 62, 65, 69, 71, 75, 78, 81, 87, 98 (top), 98 (bottom); North Wind Picture Archives, 10, 34, 44, 80, 99 (top); Corbis, 16, 19, 27; Interim Archives/Getty Images, 41, 99 (bottom); Buyenlarge/Getty Images, 59; Bettmann/Corbis, 82, 93; MPI/Getty Images, 85; Lewis W. Hine, 88; Marion Post Wolcott/Library of Congress/Getty Images, 91; LBJ Presidential Library, 94; Lynne Sladky/AP Images, 97

Editor: Kate Conley
Series Designers: Kelsey Oseid and Maggie Villaume

Cataloging-in-Publication Data

Names: Hamen, Susan E.,author.
Title: Civil War aftermath and Reconstruction / by Susan E. Hamen.
Description: Minneapolis, MN : Abdo Publishing, [2017] | Series: Essential library
    of the Civil War | Includes bibliographical references and index.
Identifiers: LCCN 2015960304 | ISBN 9781680782745 (lib. bdg.) |
    ISBN 9781680774634 (ebook)
Subjects: LCSH: Reconstruction (U.S. history. 1865-1867)--Juvenile literature. |
    United States--History--Civil War, 1861-1865--Influence--Juvenile literature.
Classification: DDC 973.8--dc23
LC record available at http://lccn.loc.gov/2015960304

CONTENTS

In 1864, the Union army destroyed an estimated 37 percent of Atlanta, Georgia.

THE FALL OF ATLANTA

Smoke rose through the night air in September 1864 as fires consumed homes and businesses in Atlanta, Georgia. Frightened citizens hurriedly packed what they could carry and fled the city. The American Civil War (1861–1865) had been raging for more than three and a half years. After a month-long siege, General William T. Sherman and the Union army had finally captured the city of Atlanta. All civilians were forced to evacuate.

For nearly four years, Atlanta had provided the Confederate army with many of the supplies it needed for the war. The city was a busy railroad hub and the industrial center of the Confederacy. General Sherman ordered every building or structure contributing to the Confederate war effort to be burned. This included mills, munitions factories, foundries, tanneries, hospitals, warehouses, and many other buildings.

Two months later, much of Atlanta lay in ruin. A Union officer wrote home to explain, "Nothing was left of Atlanta except the churches, the City Hall and private dwellings. You could hardly find a vestige of the splendid railroad depots, warehouses, etc."[1]

MARCH TO THE SEA

On November 15, Sherman and the 62,000 Union soldiers under his command left the smoldering city.[2] They began marching east through Georgia, burning the homes and barns of those who fought back. They continued until they reached the coastal city of Savannah, Georgia, on December 21.

During their 285-mile (460 km) March to the Sea, Sherman's troops destroyed railroads, wrecked supply depots, and ransacked government buildings.[3] They also stole livestock and raided homes for food. What they could not consume or

THE GATE CITY OF THE SOUTH

By the 1850s, Atlanta had become an important railway hub. Four major rail lines ran through Atlanta. Its passenger depot was the largest and finest in the South, and the volume of people passing through it helped give Atlanta the nickname the "Gate City of the South." The city's population boomed, and Atlanta became a thriving center of business. Mills, tanneries, law offices, banks, and insurance agencies began to sprout up. Immigrants made their way to Atlanta to become part of the growing city of opportunity. By 1860, approximately 12,000 people lived and worked in Atlanta.[4]

Under General Sherman's orders, soldiers destroyed railroad tracks in Atlanta.

carry with them, they burned or ruined. Their goal was to destroy everything in their path that might aid the Confederate army. They sought to frighten civilians into abandoning the cause.

Sherman was determined to make all—young and old, wealthy and poor—feel the horrors of war. To do this, he allowed his soldiers to destroy any and all property they encountered. Although Sherman had forbidden his army from harming civilians, the Union soldiers left a wake of destruction as they pressed on through Georgia. In the course of 26 days, Sherman estimated his men caused $100 million worth of damage to Georgia, which would equal approximately $1.3 billion today.[5]

GENERAL HOOD'S COMMAND

The mass destruction of Atlanta was not entirely the fault of General Sherman's troops. With supply lines to the city cut, Confederate general John Bell Hood was forced to give the command to his army to retreat and abandon Atlanta. Before leaving, he ordered his men to destroy factories and rail cars that held ammunition and other military supplies. He would rather they burn than fall into enemy hands and be used by the Union army. The explosions resulting from the fires could be heard for miles. Journalist and historian Wallace Putnam Reed described the scene, stating, "All the thunders of the universe seemed to be blazing and roaring over Atlanta."[7]

General Sherman's March to the Sea was not the only devastation endured in the course of the Civil War. Three years of battles had left cities and towns destroyed, homes and farms burned to the ground, crops devastated, tunnels and bridges collapsed, hundreds of thousands of lives lost, and a nation fractured.

DESTRUCTION AND DEVASTATION

By the end of the Civil War in 1865, nearly 50 major battles had been fought in 23 states.[6] Thousands of smaller battles, skirmishes, and engagements had occurred

General William T. Sherman rides along the Union line near Atlanta in 1864.

as well. From the moment the war began in 1861 until it ended in 1865, there were few stretches of time when there was not fighting happening somewhere in the country.

The final major engagement of the war happened on April 9, 1865, during the Battle of Appomattox Station in Virginia. The Union army had taken control of a train loaded with supplies for the Confederate army and headed a mile

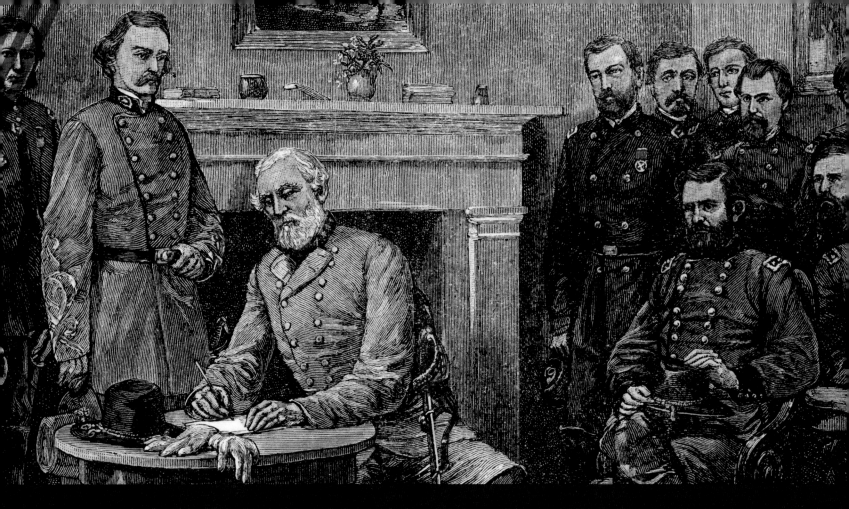

On April 9, 1865, General Lee, *left*, surrendered to General Grant, *right*, at the town of Appomattox Court House, Virginia.

north to the Confederate camp. The Confederate general Robert E. Lee realized he was outnumbered and without supplies. Realizing he had no other option, Lee ordered a truce flag to be waved. Later that day, Lee surrendered to Union general Ulysses S. Grant. It marked the end of the Civil War.

After four long years, the war had ended. It left behind death and destruction on a massive scale. President Abraham Lincoln had formulated a plan to help reconstruct, or rebuild, the United States. However, on April 14, the president was assassinated by John Wilkes Booth in Ford's Theatre in Washington, DC. Vice President Andrew Johnson, a Southerner and former slave owner who had no college education, became the new president.

"MALICE TOWARD NONE"

During President Lincoln's Second Inaugural Address on March 4, 1865, he addressed the task of Reconstruction. His plan was "To finish the work we are in; to bind up the nation's wounds; to care for him who shall have borne the battle, and for the widow, and his orphan." He continued, explaining that he wished to achieve these goals with "malice toward none; with charity for all."[8]

Without the sure leadership of President Lincoln, many wondered how the North and South would reunify successfully after such a bitter and bloody battle. Government officials sought a way for the rebellious states to peacefully rejoin the Union. Southern plantation owners wondered what would become of their mighty farms now that slavery had been abolished. Former slaves struggled to establish new, free lives, starting from nothing.

As the dust settled on the battlegrounds, the mighty problem of putting the nation back together again loomed overhead. It would take a major effort to repair the social, political, and physical effects of the Civil War. How would the United States ever recover from the bloodiest war in American history?

WAR

In the early 1800s, the United States was a growing, prospering nation. With the end of the American Revolutionary War (1775–1783), citizens turned their attention from fighting for independence to building a nation. They focused on economic, social, and governmental progress. The nation expanded in size, and more immigrants arrived in search of opportunity.

In the South, this progress centered on growing cotton. Separating the cotton fibers from the seed was a labor-intensive job. In 1793, Eli Whitney invented the cotton gin, a machine that made the process faster and easier. Widespread use of the cotton gin in the early 1800s quickly turned cotton into a lucrative cash crop for the Southern states. By the 1820s, cotton plantations had spread from Georgia to Texas.

The cotton boom required one thing for success: slave labor. Many planters had a difficult time finding enough workers to do their fieldwork because the majority opted to purchase their own land and do their own farming. Planters turned to slaves, who were unable to leave and did not have the option of purchasing land. By 1860, nearly 4 million slaves lived in the United States.[1]

THE NORTH EMBRACES ABOLITION

Northern industry did not rely on slave labor as the South did. Many Northerners began to view slavery as wrong, and wanted to end it. These people were called abolitionists. Some, such as Frederick Douglass, Harriet Beecher Stowe, and Harriet Tubman, spoke out against slavery. A movement to

NORTHERN INDUSTRY

In the North, people had transitioned their economy from agriculture to manufacturing. After 1820, cities such as New York City, New York; Boston, Massachusetts; Philadelphia, Pennsylvania; and Baltimore, Maryland, expanded and became centers of industry. In the following decades, these cities and the manufacturing centers that surrounded them accounted for 25 percent of the nation's manufacturing.[2] The majority of the nation's printing and publishing, as well as the manufacturing of glass, drugs, paints, textiles, musical instruments, furniture, hardware, and machinery, happened in these cities. As the Civil War raged on, the Northern economy grew. The North had the industrial expertise and workforce to produce supplies needed for war, including weapons, leather goods, iron products, and textiles.

make slaveholding illegal in the United States gained popularity in the North. This threatened the plantation-based economy and lifestyle that had spread throughout the South. Cotton plantations brought great wealth to their owners. In 1860, three-fifths of the wealthiest people in the United States lived in the South.[3] Slavery was not going to end without a fight from the Southern states.

As territories became states, Congress carefully balanced the number of slave states versus free states. This changed in 1850, when California was admitted as a free state, but no slave states were added to balance it out. Then in 1860, Abraham Lincoln was elected president. He belonged to the Republican Party, which was against slavery. Southerners worried they would be outnumbered. Some believed their only option was to secede from the United States. In the months that followed Lincoln's election, seven states (South Carolina, Mississippi, Florida, Alabama, Georgia, Louisiana, and Texas) left the Union and formed the Confederate States of America.

WAR ERUPTS

As each Southern state seceded from the Union, it seized control of any federal forts within its borders. On April 12, 1861, the Confederate army fired on Fort Sumter, a US military post on an island in the harbor of Charleston, South Carolina. The following day, Major Robert Anderson surrendered to Confederate general P. G. T. Beauregard. This marked the beginning of the American Civil

For two days, Confederates fired on Fort Sumter. The fort was out of supplies and

War. In the weeks that followed, Virginia, Arkansas, Tennessee, and North Carolina also left the Union and joined the Confederacy. President Lincoln declared these states were not a sovereign nation, but rather states in an act of rebellion.

The country was plunged into a four-year war that tore the nation apart. The death toll rose to approximately 620,000 soldiers by the time the war came to an end in 1865. No other war would claim as many American lives.[4] Another 476,000 soldiers were wounded, and an estimated 60,000 surgeries were performed in makeshift military hospitals to amputate injured limbs.[5]

"LIKE DEMONS THEY RUSH IN"

Southern widow Dolly Lunt Burge, a wealthy plantation owner in Covington, Georgia, recorded in her journal her experience when Union soldiers barged onto her land and raided her plantation:

But like Demons they rush in. My yards are full. To my smoke house, my Dairy, Pantry, kitchen & cellar like famished wolves they come, breaking locks & whatever is in their way. The thousand pounds of meat in my smoke house is gone in a twinkling, my flour, my meal, my lard, butter, eggs, pickles of various kinds. . . . My eighteen fat turkeys, my hens, chickens, & fowls. My young pigs are shot down in my yard, & hunted as if they were the rebels themselves.[6]

SHERMAN'S WARFARE

Sherman was not eager to slaughter Confederate troops on the battlefield. Prior to the war, he had been friends with men who became Confederate military leaders. Sherman believed that his plan of total destruction would hurt Southern morale so badly it would hasten the end of the war and therefore reduce the number of casualties. As he saw it, the enemy army was sustained by the will of the people. If he could crush the civilians, the Confederacy would fold. "We cannot change the hearts of these people of the South," he explained, "but we can make war so terrible . . . and make them so *sick* of war that generations [will] pass away before they again appeal to it."[7]

DESTRUCTION

In addition to the staggering number of dead and wounded, large swaths of the country lay in ruins, especially in the South. Homes, farms, and businesses were hit by stray artillery or burned down during nearby battles. Enemy troops overtook and destroyed many properties. Sometimes people deliberately set fire to public buildings to prevent them from falling into enemy hands.

Personal property was not spared from this destruction. Furniture, rugs, silverware, dishes, linens, and other household goods were often stolen or destroyed. Soldiers pillaged food from pantries and root cellars. They would arrive at a plantation and burn thousands of bales of cotton, confiscate livestock, destroy carriages, steal household goods, and even empty inkwells. Historians estimate that the loss of property in the South, due to destruction of physical property, equaled one-third to two-thirds

Women of the Confederacy struggled to protect their homes and property during the war. At the war's end, most Southern women had been reduced to living in poverty, and more than 70,000 were left as widows.

of all Confederate wealth.[8] Another large portion of Southern wealth vanished when slaves—formerly considered valuable property—were emancipated.

With the men off to war, women were ill prepared to defend themselves and their property. They watched as advancing enemy soldiers ransacked their homes. Many tried to hide property in wells, cellars, fields, or even mattresses. Soldiers ripped apart houses, barns, and gardens looking for valuables. Some women believed they could hide smaller items such as jewelry in their petticoats or under their dresses, but their bodies were searched. Women could do nothing to stop troops from stealing their possessions, consuming their food, and then destroying houses and barns before they left. In the wake of the soldiers, women and children were left homeless and penniless.

As troops marched across the land and engaged in battles, they destroyed and burned fields and crops. Soldiers removed fences as they crossed private land. During Sherman's March to the Sea, the South's infrastructure received massive damage. Sherman's troops demolished rail lines, heating the tracks and wrapping them around trees. They seized railroad depots and cut telegraph lines, hindering communication throughout the South. Many bridges lay in ruin after being blown up, and roadways were left in impassable condition.

The Confederacy was simply not able to absorb such massive losses. Southern plantations had lost a large part of their workforce when the slaves were freed. The war had also depleted many Southerners of their wealth, as much of it was measured in the number of slaves they owned. In fact, in 1860, the economic value of all slaves owned surpassed the combined invested value of all railroads, factories, and banks in the nation.[9]

AFTER THE SMOKE CLEARS

When the war came to an end and Southern soldiers returned to their homes, they found chimneys in overgrown fields where homes once stood. Most fields had gone unplanted for four years and were in shambles. There was much work to be done, but no workers to help with it. The majority of landowners had no money to pay workers anyway.

Money itself was a massive problem in the South. At the onset of the war, the Confederacy had designed and released its own paper currency. A total of $1.7 billion worth of Confederate bank notes were circulated.[10] At the beginning of the war, the currency was accepted throughout the South for the purchase of goods and to pay wages.

As the conflict dragged on, people began to doubt the success of the Confederacy. The currency depreciated and prices soared. By 1865, Southerners were paying as much as $50 in Confederate notes for a cake of soap (approximately $800 today). A man's suit

CONFEDERATE CURRENCY

The newly formed Confederate States of America designed, printed, and issued its own paper bank notes. With each passing year of the war, Confederate currency depreciated. It was so worthless that many people bartered or wrote promises to pay at a later date. When the war ended, Confederate currency could no longer be used. Some people burned it as waste paper. Those who had large amounts of it lost much wealth.

ran as high as $2,700 (approximately $42,000 today).[11] The money had become nearly worthless.

BITTERNESS AND RESENTMENT

With many of their homes and plantations burned, their possessions gone, their money worthless, and no jobs to be found, the future looked bleak for those in the South. Southerners felt a deep bitterness toward the North. Their plantation economy and way of life had been destroyed. Many believed the Southern states had lost their identities and their culture.

In addition to the loss of homes, many businesses that supported daily life were damaged or gone. Shops, markets, post offices, courthouses, and stables had become the victims of war, further weakening the Southern economy. Several hospitals, clinics, churches, and other public service organizations were no longer able to help those in need.

Whereas Southerners resented the destruction the Union army had left behind, many Northerners wanted revenge on the South for seceding and causing a war that resulted in the loss of more than half a million lives.

In 1865, when the war finally came to an end, there was much repairing to be done. Not only did countless towns and buildings have to be rebuilt, but the economy of the South had to be addressed as well. The nation's Constitution and laws were in need of amending and rewriting to address the political and social

Women in Southern cities, such as Richmond, Virginia, felt bitter toward the Union soldiers they saw in their streets.

changes that had occurred. The rights of newly freed slaves had to be addressed, and the nation needed to provide assistance to them as they built free lives. In addition, a fractured nation had to somehow be made whole again.

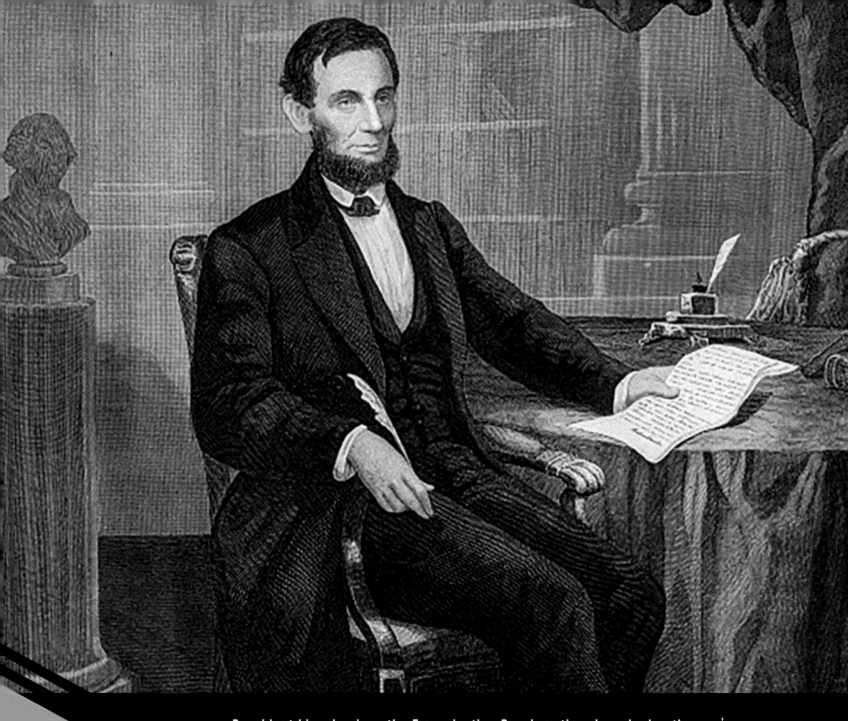

President Lincoln signs the Emancipation Proclamation, broadening the war's focus from only saving the Union to also freeing the slaves.

LINCOLN'S RECONSTRUCTION

President Lincoln's war efforts began to broaden in late 1862. He wanted not only to save the Union, but also to end slavery. On September 22, 1862, Lincoln issued a preliminary announcement. It stated the seceded states had to return to the Union before the New Year or Lincoln would declare their slaves free. When no states rejoined the Union, Lincoln issued the Emancipation Proclamation on January 1, 1863.

The Emancipation Proclamation formally ended slavery in states that had rebelled against the Union. The Union army was no longer fighting only to save the Union. With the Emancipation Proclamation, the war turned into a crusade for human freedom.

The proclamation also declared the Union would recruit African Americans to be soldiers for limited positions in the military. Nearly 180,000 former slaves enlisted and joined the fight to end slavery.[1]

Although Northerners sought an end to slavery, not all Northern politicians agreed on how freed slaves should be treated. The Radical Republicans were a group of people who pushed for freedom and equal rights for freed slaves. Moderates and conservatives believed slaves should be freed but did not think they should share the same rights as whites. The future for African Americans was uncertain as Northerners grappled with what to do with newly freed slaves.

EMANCIPATION VERSUS ABOLITION

President Lincoln issued the Emancipation Proclamation on January 1, 1863. However, it freed slaves only in Confederate states. It did not officially change the US laws about slavery. Many questioned the legality of the proclamation. In 1865, the Thirteenth Amendment abolished slavery permanently by amending the Constitution of the United States. It made slavery illegal throughout the United States.

THE TEN PERCENT PLAN

Radical Republicans called for Southern states to be punished for their rebellion. However, President Lincoln did not want to punish the South. Instead, he wanted to come up with a plan that would ensure an end to slavery everywhere and effectively put the country back together. He believed it was important

Citizens of South Carolina take the oath of allegiance to the United States of America after the war.

that prominent Confederate leaders were not allowed to be part of new state governments in Southern states once they were admitted back into the Union.

On December 8, 1863, Lincoln issued the Proclamation of Amnesty and Reconstruction, which was also referred to as the Ten Percent Plan. It marked the start of Reconstruction for the United States. It outlined Lincoln's lenient plan that he hoped would be enticing enough to rebel states that it would help reunite the Union and the Confederacy.

The proclamation had three main points. First, it granted the citizens of seceded states amnesty. It restored the property of most people, with the exception of high-ranking officials and military leaders. Second, it required only 10 percent of all eligible voters counted in a state's 1860 census to take an oath

A TEST CASE

Louisiana was the first state to implement the Ten Percent Plan. Lincoln selected General Nathaniel P. Banks to oversee Louisiana's new government. Banks organized the state's elections for February 1864.

In the following months, leaders worked on a new state constitution. According to historian Eric Foner, they were "reform-minded professionals, small businessmen, artisans, civil servants, and a sprinkling of farmers and laborers. The planter class, which, as one delegate put it, had governed the state 'for the sole and exclusive benefit of slaveholders,' was conspicuous by its absence."[2]

The state's constitution passed in May 1864, but it did not grant African Americans the right to vote. This angered members of the US Congress. They refused to accept Louisiana's electoral votes in the 1864 presidential election. Louisiana's new government faltered and fell apart.

of allegiance to the United States before a new state government was initiated. Third, readmitted states had to come up with a plan for handling newly freed slaves without compromising their freedom.

This Ten Percent Plan allowed states to rejoin the Union without extreme difficulty, requiring only one-tenth of voters to swear allegiance to the United States. It appealed to the rebel states. This was part of Lincoln's goal. He believed if his plan were too difficult or harsh, states would refuse to return to the Union. Lincoln's Ten Percent Plan allowed citizens of readmitted states to have the same rights and privileges as citizens of loyal states.

NO PARDON FOR SOME

Lincoln's Ten Percent Plan called for full pardons to those who swore allegiance to the Union. However, this did not include high Confederate officials, army and navy officers, US judges, or any congressmen who left their posts to fight for or otherwise aid the South. They were excluded from Lincoln's pardon.

OPPOSITION

Radical Republicans believed Lincoln's plan wasn't harsh enough and did not prevent those who had caused the war from returning to power. Both Republicans and Democrats in the North feared Lincoln's plan would result in Confederates signing the oath and then returning to their old ways.

One Radical Republican, Thaddeus Stevens, viewed Lincoln's plan as too forgiving. He argued the Southern states were conquered provinces, not states.

RADICAL REPUBLICANS

The Radical Republicans were a political party that opposed slavery. During Reconstruction, they believed the only way to restore the nation was to have freed slaves equal to whites under the law. They also wanted leaders of the Confederacy punished for their role in Civil War.

One of the best known Radical Republicans was Charles Sumner. The senator from Massachusetts argued Southern states had "committed suicide" when they seceded.

He wanted to completely reorganize Southern society. Sumner favored giving freed slaves parcels of their former masters' land. Sumner also wanted states to create a public school system open to children of all races.

These views were at odds with President Johnson, who favored a more lenient approach to Reconstruction. As a result, Sumner and other Radical Republicans supported President Johnson's impeachment.

According to Stevens, this meant Congress could enact whatever changes it liked. He and other radicals also wanted all Confederate supporters excluded from the new government. As they saw it, only men who had never supported the Confederacy should be allowed to take part in government.

Further, it was the goal of Radical Republicans to amend the US Constitution to protect the rights of freed slaves, or freedmen, and make them equal citizens. Stevens believed freedmen should have the right to vote. Moderate Republicans believed strongly in the superiority of a capitalist system based on wage labor, and they wanted to see blacks protected from conditions that resembled slavery. But they did not support making African Americans equal citizens and did not believe they should vote or serve on juries.

Democrats, on the other hand, opposed all of the goals of the Republican Party. Lincoln tried to work with Congress to get the support of the majority. But his vision was clear, and he proceeded with the Ten Percent Plan in states that had been occupied by Union troops. He did so without the approval of Congress, arguing he could use his pardoning power as president and did not need congressional approval.

THE WADE-DAVIS BILL

On May 4, 1864, a bill written by Representative Henry Winter Davis of Maryland and Senator Benjamin Wade of Ohio was passed in the House by a vote of 73 to 59.[3] It passed in the Senate on July 2 of the same year. The Wade-Davis Reconstruction Bill required at least 50 percent of eligible voters in each state to take an "ironclad" oath swearing their allegiance to the US Constitution.

With that completed, the state could call a constitutional convention. To be considered for readmittance to the Union, these state constitutional conventions were required to abolish slavery in that state.

Lincoln disagreed with the strict terms of Reconstruction outlined in the Wade-Davis Bill. He wanted to keep the reunification more flexible, and he believed the bill would postpone Reconstruction until after the war had ended. He also worried it would undo progress in Louisiana and Arkansas, which had already worked toward becoming states again. Lincoln believed restoring states to the Union would encourage other states to lay down their arms and return to the Union. He pocket vetoed the bill, meaning he did not sign the bill after Congress had adjourned. Therefore, the bill did not become law.

President Lincoln rejected the Wade-Davis Bill because he did not want to abolish slavery with a federal law. Rather, he wanted Congress to pass an amendment, changing the US Constitution to abolish slavery.

Wade and Davis were unhappy with the president's actions. They drafted the Wade-Davis Manifesto, which was published in newspapers. In it, they accused the president of overstepping his power. "The President, by preventing this bill from becoming a law," they explained, "holds the electoral votes of the rebel States at the dictation of his personal ambition."[4] In essence, among other things, Wade and Davis were saying that voters in these newly reunified states would owe their allegiance to Lincoln and would therefore vote for him in the next election.

POCKETING THE BILL

A bill must go through specific steps outlined in the US Constitution to become a law. A bill must be voted on and approved by both the House of Representatives and the Senate. After passing through Congress, the president has ten days to sign the bill or veto it. The bill automatically becomes law if the president does neither of these. However, if Congress gives a bill to the president less than ten days before the end of a congressional session, there is an exception. If the president ignores it, it does not become law. This is called a pocket veto.

THE THIRTEENTH AMENDMENT

Lincoln worked with Republicans on the Thirteenth Amendment, which would change the US Constitution. It would officially end slavery on all US soil. On April 8, 1864, the Senate passed the amendment, but Democrats in the House of Representatives defeated it.

Despite the opposition Lincoln faced in Congress, he was reelected to a second term on November 8, 1864. During that election, more Republicans won seats in the House. As a result, on January 31, 1865, the House passed the amendment 119 to 56.[5]

The House erupted in cheers when the amendment passed. Freedmen in the gallery who had come to witness the vote cheered as well. The Republicans had claimed a great victory for African Americans. In celebration, a 100-gun salute with cannons was set off in Washington, DC, to commemorate the occasion.

Lincoln signed his approval on February 1, 1865. The amendment read:

Neither slavery nor involuntary servitude, except as a punishment for crime whereof the party shall have been duly convicted, shall exist within the United States, or any place subject to their jurisdiction.

Congress shall have power to enforce this article by appropriate legislation.[6]

A moment of pride and celebration took place in US House of Representatives when the Thirteenth Amendment was enacted.

After Congress passed the amendment and Lincoln signed it, two-thirds of the states had to ratify it. That happened by the end of the year, and on December 6, 1865, the Thirteenth Amendment was made part of the US Constitution. Slavery was finally officially abolished.

THADDEUS STEVENS

1792–1868

Thaddeus Stevens was an outspoken Radical Republican leader during Reconstruction. Stevens was a lawyer from Vermont. He was passionately opposed to slavery, and he had a great distrust of the wealthy upper class.

Stevens began representing Pennsylvania in the US House of Representatives in 1848. He was well-spoken and quickly became a leader. During the Civil War, he supported harsh measures again the South as well as freeing all slaves.

After the war, Stevens and other Radical Republicans strongly disagreed with President Johnson on how to reconstruct the South. Stevens drafted the resolution to impeach Johnson in 1868. Less than six months later, Stevens died.

Andrew Johnson, *fourth from left*, received news of Lincoln's death at 7:22 a.m. on April 15, 1865. Less than three hours later, he took the oath of office.

JOHNSON'S RECONSTRUCTION

In April 1865, it was not yet clear whether Lincoln would stick to his vision for Reconstruction or if he would compromise and move toward the Radical Republicans' hope for Reconstruction. The country would not witness how he would have proceeded, because on April 14, 1865, President Lincoln was shot at Ford's Theatre in Washington, DC, by Confederate sympathizer John Wilkes Booth. Lincoln died the following day.

Northerners wept when they heard the news. African Americans were devastated when they learned of the death of the man who had worked to end slavery. General Grant broke down and cried while standing over the president's coffin in Washington, DC.

Shortly after taking office, President Johnson offered pardons to all rebels except for their leaders. Johnson's actions outraged Radical Republicans.

Many Northerners wanted revenge on the South for Lincoln's murder. One Union soldier wrote in a letter dated April 18, 1865, "Father we have heard that President Lincoln has been killed by some traitor in Washington. If that is true I say that we ought to hang every damn rebel in the Southern Confederacy. . . . I tell you it is a very hard blow for this nation to lose our President at this present time."[1]

In the South, however, some newspapers reported Lincoln's death as "GLORIOUS NEWS!"[2] The *Chattanooga Daily Rebel* boldly stated, "Abe has gone to answer before the bar of God for the innocent blood which he has permitted to be shed."[3]

A NEW PRESIDENT TAKES THE HELM

As Northerners mourned the death of Lincoln, Vice President Andrew Johnson was sworn in as the next president. Johnson had been raised in the South. Many wondered if Johnson would move forward with President Lincoln's plan for Reconstruction or create one of his own.

Lincoln had been able to reach agreements with the radical Republicans. It looked as though it would be more challenging for Johnson. He was a Democrat with ties to the South. Many doubted Johnson could peacefully manage Reconstruction. A sharp division grew between the president and Congress.

PRESIDENTIAL RECONSTRUCTION

Throughout the war, Congress had met continuously. At the war's end, members of Congress took an eight-month break. During these months, President Johnson made plans for Reconstruction without the approval of Congress.

On May 29, 1865, Johnson issued a proclamation granting amnesty to Confederate soldiers who pledged their loyalty to the Constitution. High-ranking officers and wealthy Southerners were not included under this plan, but they could appeal to Johnson individually. He handed out approximately

7,000 pardons.[4] All land and property, except slaves, were returned to their prewar owners.

Another proclamation addressed new state governments. Once a state ratified the Thirteenth Amendment and ended its ties with the Confederacy, leaders could reorganize their state governments. Many ex-Confederates were voted back into office. Outspoken Confederates were finding their way back into Southern politics.

Ex-Confederates passed new laws that limited the rights of African Americans. These Black Codes, as they were called, targeted former slaves. African Americans could be fined or imprisoned for things as simple as an insulting gesture. Some laws allowed freedmen to be arrested for vagrancy if they did not have a job. If the person could not pay the fine, the sheriff could hire him out to any white person willing to pay the fine. Johnson did nothing to stop the Black Codes.

CONGRESS REACTS

Northerners were furious. They believed Southern states had reelected Confederate wartime leaders to office and reestablished a form of slavery through the Black Codes. In December 1865, when Congress reconvened, Northern Republicans forbade the Southern representatives from participating in Congress.

Under the Black Codes, free African-American men could be sold to pay unfair fines.

Congress took control of Reconstruction by passing the Wade-Davis Bill Lincoln had pocket vetoed. Now, before a state could be readmitted to the Union, Congress expected 50 percent of its voters to make the "ironclad" oath of loyalty.[5] The Republican-dominated Congress also wanted to give the freed slaves the freedoms and rights it believed everyone deserved.

Not all of Congress's plans went smoothly, though. In 1866, it renewed the Freedman's Bureau Bill, which helped transition the South from slavery to freedom. Despite Congress's approval, President Johnson vetoed the bill. He believed the bill allowed the federal government to overtake rights that belonged to the states. Members of Congress overrode Johnson's veto, passing the bill.

CIVIL RIGHTS AND AN AMENDMENT

On April 9, 1866, Congress passed the Civil Rights Act. This guaranteed citizenship to all people born in the United States, with the exception of Native Americans who were not subject to US law. It also stated all citizens had equal rights. Johnson vetoed the bill, but Congress overrode Johnson and the bill became law.

As US citizens, freed slaves were now able to enter into contracts, sue, and testify in court. They could purchase, inherit, sell, lease, or transfer ownership of personal property. The Civil Rights Act also made Black Codes illegal. Those who interfered with these new rights of African Americans could be jailed up to one year or fined up to $1,000.[6]

Congress pressed on, passing the Fourteenth Amendment in June 1886. It granted full citizenship to all people "born or naturalized in the United States." This included former slaves. The amendment also declared the North was not responsible for Confederate debts. Plantation owners could not sue the US government for the wealth they had lost when their slaves were freed.

The Fourteenth Amendment also took away some powers from the president. He could no longer pardon former Confederates. Now, any former Confederates who wanted to hold public office needed a congressional pardon, which required a two-thirds majority vote.

Before the Fourteenth Amendment could take effect, three-quarters of all the states had to ratify it. Some states ratified it right away, while others took much longer. The amendment was finally added to the US Constitution on July 9, 1868.

RIOTS

As Johnson and Congress argued about Reconstruction, problems grew in some Southern cities. Throughout the war, the African-American population in Memphis, Tennessee, had quadrupled, which led to racial tensions. In May 1866, a riot erupted in Memphis between white policemen and African-American soldiers, lasting three days. Forty-six African Americans and two whites were

NEW VOTERS

Because Tennessee was readmitted to the Union in 1866 before the Reconstruction Acts were enacted, it became the first state to hold an election with African-American voters. The Tennessee gubernatorial election of 1867 marked the first election in US history in which Southern African Americans were allowed to vote. According to the *National Intelligencer* newspaper, 56,022 whites and 37,216 African Americans were registered to vote. Military personnel were posted in Tennessee to ensure peace. Fortunately, things ran smoothly at the polls that day.[7]

The riots in Memphis increased sympathies for freed slaves among leaders in the US Congress.

dead, and hundreds of homes, schools, and churches owned by African Americans had been vandalized or burned by rampaging whites.

New Orleans, Louisiana, experienced rioting as well when whites attacked a peaceful political meeting, leaving many African Americans dead. Republican Louisiana governor James Madison Wells banned Confederates from voting, while working toward obtaining voting rights for African-American men. A riot in the street left 34 African Americans and three white Republicans dead. Hundreds more were injured.[8]

IMPEACHMENT

The passing of the Civil Rights Act and the Fourteenth Amendment ushered in the period of Radical Reconstruction. It was a time of heated disagreements between the president and Congress. On March 2, 1867, Congress overrode two of Johnson's vetoes. One was for the first Reconstruction Act and the other was for the Tenure of Office Act.

Under the Reconstruction Act, ten ex-Confederate states were divided into five military districts. The eleventh Confederate state, Tennessee, was exempt since it had already ratified the Fourteenth Amendment and had been readmitted to the Union. A Union general was assigned to each district. States could be readmitted to the Union after ratifying the Fourteenth Amendment and approving new state constitutions that allowed adult African-American men to vote.

The Tenure of Office Act restricted the president's ability to fire cabinet officials without Senate approval. Johnson wanted to test the act, so in August 1867 Johnson fired Secretary of War Edwin Stanton without the Senate's approval. Congress was not in session at the time. When it reconvened, the House of Representatives moved to impeach Johnson. On February 24, 1868, the

House voted 126 to 47 in favor of impeaching President Johnson.[9] He was to be tried before the Senate.

In March, Thaddeus Stevens and Benjamin Butler led the prosecution against the president. Stevens spoke harshly against Johnson's actions. After 11 weeks, the Senate fell short by one vote to impeach Johnson. The president remained in office until the end of his term, but he agreed to stop actively obstructing Republican Reconstruction policies while he remained in office.

MAKING CHANGES

The Reconstruction Acts brought change to the South. Hundreds of thousands of African-American men registered as voters and took to the polls for the 1868 election. Most voted for Republicans. A large number of white Southern men chose not to vote, as they refused to participate in an election that allowed African Americans to vote. As a result, the 1868 election win went to the Republican candidate, General Ulysses S. Grant. Republicans also won control of many Southern state governments.

With the help of these new leaders, by 1868 seven Southern states had completed the requirements for readmittance to the Union. Alabama, Arkansas, Florida, Georgia, Louisiana, North Carolina, and South Carolina were welcomed back. Two years later, Mississippi, Virginia, and Texas were restored to the Union.

Johnson's impeachment trial

On February 3, 1870, the Fifteenth Amendment to the US Constitution was ratified. It prohibited states from taking away the right to vote based on race, color, or prior enslavement. The amendment did not, however, prohibit states from instituting voter qualifications. Poll taxes and literacy tests prevented many African Americans from being able to vote.

In the summer of 1870, Charles Sumner introduced the final and most ambitious Reconstruction law. This was the Civil Rights Act, which eventually passed on March 1, 1875. It protected the rights of all Americans, regardless of race. Access to restaurants, theaters, and public transportation could not be denied anyone because of race. The act was not enforced, however, and the Supreme Court later declared it unconstitutional.

AMNESTY PROCLAMATION

During the final weeks of the war, Jefferson Davis, the president of the Confederacy, had been captured in Georgia. Davis was charged with treason, a crime punishable by hanging. Davis's attorneys asked for a dismissal in early December 1868, claiming the Fourteenth Amendment had already punished Davis because it prevented him from holding a public office. Further penalties, they argued, would violate the Fifth Amendment, which prevents a person from being punished multiple times for the same crime. The US Supreme Court was divided. Before it reached a decision, President Johnson issued the Amnesty Proclamation on December 25, 1868. It granted a pardon to all who had fought in the rebellion. This included Davis.

TENURE OF OFFICE ACT

Johnson tested the Tenure of Office Act when he dismissed Secretary of War Edwin Stanton. Stanton was an ally of the Radical Republicans, and Johnson did not want him in the cabinet any longer. Johnson dismissed Stanton. He believed the Tenure of Office Act was unconstitutional. Johnson sought to force the act to be tried in court. Instead, he found himself standing trial. In 1926, the US Supreme Court declared the act to be unconstitutional.

ANDREW JOHNSON

1808–1875

Andrew Johnson was born on December 29, 1808, in Raleigh, North Carolina. He later moved to Tennessee and started a tailoring business. He became successful enough to purchase land and slaves.

Johnson had complex views on slavery. He believed slaves were inferior to their white owners. However, Johnson disliked the wealthy and powerful slave owners who controlled Tennessee.

Johnson was elected mayor of Greeneville, Tennessee, in 1834, and was elected to the US House of Representatives in 1843. When Tennessee seceded in 1860, Johnson broke with his state. He was the only Southern senator who remained loyal to the Union throughout the Civil War. Johnson saw secession as a way to protect the state's elite.

Johnson was elected as vice president in 1864. He became the seventeenth president after Abraham Lincoln's death in April 1865. After a failed impeachment trial, Johnson finished his term. He returned to Tennessee in 1869 and won election to the US Senate in 1874. The next year, Johnson died.

RECONSTRUCTION FOR AFRICAN AMERICANS

For former slaves, freedom was bittersweet. They were no longer forced to work without pay or held against their will. However, many slaves had been separated from their families when their owners sold them. Slaves that had been sold were often never seen by family members again.

After emancipation, many former slaves hoped to improve their lives. They tried to reunite their families, and they built new communities. Couples legalized their marriages. Some adopted new names for their new start in a free world, and some families moved out of the South entirely. Former slaves could finally make their own decisions and pursue a better life.

During Reconstruction, freed slaves viewed education as a key to improving their lives. New schools opened all over the South, and students ranged from the elderly to small children.

African Americans faced the challenge of finding homes and jobs. Although many endured severe hardships on plantations, they were provided with food and shelter. Now they had nowhere to live, slim prospects for finding employment, and few possessions. Many moved from rural areas to cities in the hope of finding employment. They also believed it was safer in cities where Union soldiers were stationed and could offer a small amount of protection.

Churches helped set up schools for former slaves. Many African Americans viewed education, which had been denied to slaves, as a crucial step to a better life. Prior to emancipation, it had been illegal in the South to teach slaves to read. Booker T. Washington, a famous African American educator, orator, and author, noted, "It was a whole race trying to go to school. Few were too young, and none too old, to make the attempt to learn. As fast as any kind of teachers could be secured, not only were day-schools filled, but night-schools as well."[1]

EMANCIPATION AND THE CHURCH

At the time of emancipation, many churches attempted to help newly freed slaves. Northern African-American leaders established missions and schools in the South. These efforts, along with new public schools, increased literacy rates among African Americans. They rose from 5 percent in 1870 to approximately 70 percent by 1900.[2]

Northern churches also brought their style of worship to the South. They urged ex-slaves to give up the influences of African practices, such as drumming and dancing, for a more formal style of worship. They argued that "true" Christianity was more calm and dignified. Many African Americans in urban areas changed their worship to match customs of the Northern churches. In rural areas, however, freed slaves often kept their traditional styles of worship.

SERVING THEIR COUNTRY

Prior to Reconstruction, some freed slaves chose military service in the Union army during the Civil War. Enlisting in the army provided them with food, shelter, medical care, basic education, and a paycheck.

But serving in the army was not without risk. Jefferson Davis, president of the Confederacy, issued a proclamation regarding former slaves who were serving as soldiers. In it he said these soldiers were not honorable fighters but were "robbers and criminals deserving death, and that they and each of them be whenever captured reserved for execution."[3]

Despite these risks, by the war's end approximately 179,000 African Americans served in the US Army. They constituted 10 percent of the Union army. Another 19,000 served in the US Navy.[4]

THE FIFTY-FOURTH MASSACHUSETTS REGIMENT

The first call for African-American soldiers came from Massachusetts governor John A. Andrew in February 1863. Eager to help abolish slavery, volunteers came from New York, Indiana, Ohio, Canada, and even the Caribbean. The regiment had 1,007 African-American soldiers and 37 white officers.[5]

On July 18, 1863, the regiment led an assault on Fort Wagner in South Carolina. It was a brutal battle. Almost half of the regiment was killed, wounded, or went missing. Sergeant William H. Carney earned the Congressional Medal of Honor for his contributions to the battle, making him the first African American with this honor.

Before Fort Wagner, many people had been skeptical about the success of an African-American army unit. The soldiers of the Fifty-Fourth showed bravery and patriotism, never surrendering despite the hardships. Its success led the army to create other African-American units.

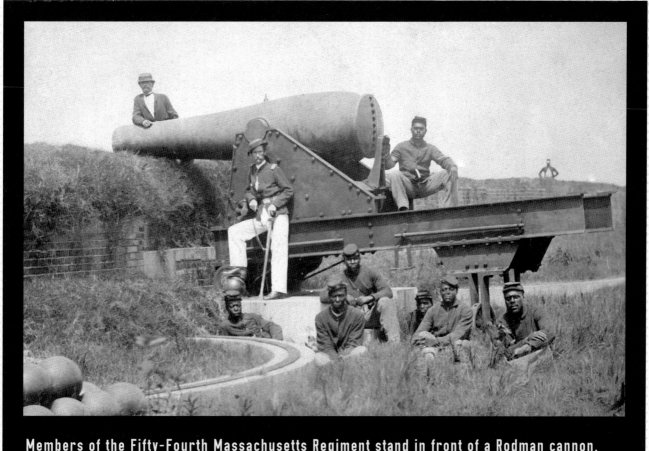
Members of the Fifty-Fourth Massachusetts Regiment stand in front of a Rodman cannon.

THE FREEDMEN'S BUREAU

The war created an immense refugee population of freed African-American slaves and impoverished and displaced whites in the South. On March 3, 1865, Congress established the Bureau of Refugees, Freedmen, and Abandoned Lands,

This engraving from 1866 shows African Americans lined up outside the Freedmen's Bureau in Richmond, Virginia.

commonly known as the Freedmen's Bureau. The bureau provided food, housing, clothing, medical aid, and legal assistance to freedmen and white refugees in the South. It also helped African Americans transition from their lives of slavery to freedom. This often included trying to protect them against violence from resentful white Southerners.

The organization attempted to settle freed slaves on Confederate land that had either been abandoned or seized during the war. It also built 4,300 schools that educated 250,000 students, constructed several hospitals, and established a few colleges. Between 1865 and 1870, the bureau spent nearly $5 million to educate former slaves, the equivalent of approximately $75 million today.[6]

For all the good the Freedmen's Bureau attempted to do, it was understaffed. The bureau's commissioner, Major General Oliver O. Howard, and his staff of 901 workers could not keep up with the needs of 4 million freed slaves.[7] Despite the enormous achievements of the Freedmen's Bureau, white Southerners pressured Congress to shut it down. In 1870, the bureau was forced to close its doors.

FINDING FAMILY

The Freedmen's Bureau tried to help freed slaves find their family members by placing ads in newspapers. Preachers read the ads aloud in church services, and they were also placed in more than 800 post offices in the South. One freed slave placed an ad searching for her children:

Dear Editor—I wish to find my four children. I was sold away from them in 1859, to Jack Simmons, then a farmer and blacksmith in Howard county. . . . My name was then Hannah Simmons; my husband was Juba D. Lacy. We had four children. The oldest was then 7 years named Lycingus, next Jerry, Jordan, and Jim. I was sold to Sam Brown. . . . He brought me to Mississippi, and sold me to Judge Hill. I still live in Canton, Mississippi.[8]

—Emma Emory

FORTY ACRES AND A MULE

When General Sherman ended his March to the Sea in late 1864, he established a headquarters in Savannah, Georgia. There, he and Secretary of War Edwin M. Stanton met with a group of African-American leaders. They discussed how to provide for the vast number of African Americans who had entered Sherman's lines on his march to Savannah.

During the discussion, an idea was born. Sherman and Stanton had asked these leaders what the African Americans would like for themselves. Baptist minister Garrison Frazier answered, "The way we can best take care of ourselves is to have land, and turn it and till it by our own labor . . . and we can soon maintain ourselves and have something to spare. . . . We want to be placed on land until we are able to buy it and make it our own."[9]

This request became General Sherman's Special Field Order No. 15. Issued on January 16, 1865, the order called for freedmen to receive 40 acres (16 ha) of tillable land. It divided 400,000 acres (16,000 ha) of land along the coastline from Charleston, South Carolina, to Saint John's River in Florida. This large strip of abandoned and confiscated land was to be redistributed to newly freed slaves. Later, Sherman requested the army lend mules to the new settlers to assist with plowing and planting.

Newly freed African Americans sought land that would let them build their lives in the post-slavery era.

Freedmen rushed to take advantage of Sherman's order. But in the fall of 1865, Johnson overturned the order. Much of the land that had been promised to former slaves was returned to its original owners if they returned to claim it.

The US government struggled with rebuilding a nation that could successfully offer African Americans a solid start in their new lives of freedom. Although they were no longer slaves, they experienced a great deal of hardship.

MOVING WEST
FREEDOM ON THE PRAIRIE

During Reconstruction, thousands of freed slaves decided to move west. Many chose to go to Kansas. The state had a strong tradition of abolitionism. It also had thousands of acres of land available for Americans regardless of race.

Benjamin "Pap" Singleton, a former slave, wrote a document called *The Advantage of Living in a Free State* in 1874. In it, he encouraged former slaves to move to Kansas. Between 1874 and 1890, Kansas received more than 10,000 former slaves.[10]

A group of freed slaves from Kentucky established the settlement of Nicodemus in Kansas. It is the only surviving settlement of its kind. Residents built a school, churches, and a post office. Business leaders created hotels, lumberyards, drugstores, general stores, and an ice cream parlor. To relax, residents could join the town's baseball team, literary society, or band.

Life in Nicodemus and similar settlements was difficult. The settlers lived in dugout shelters and faced harsh weather and barren fields. In Topeka, Kansas, the mayor refused to spend any of the city's money to help the new settlers. For many slaves, however, this harsh new life was preferable to the South. A Topeka newspaper called *The Colored Citizen* said, "it is better to starve to death in Kansas than be shot and killed in the South."[11]

Settlers stand in front of their new house in Nicodemus, Kansas. In 1996, Congress named Nicodemus a National Historic Site.

The war damaged many homes. Confederate sharpshooters used this Atlanta home as a base until Union forces damaged it.

COMING HOME

Reconstruction encompassed more than adjusting to emancipation. There was also the matter of helping veterans who had spent the last four years fighting for either the Union or Confederate cause. As the war drew to a close in 1865, hundreds of thousands of Union and Confederate soldiers returned home.

Returning home was not easy. Many veterans in the South found their houses gone or in ruins and the land devastated. Many women and children had been displaced in the course of the war. Families and homes were in need of rebuilding. In addition, one in 13 Civil War veterans had one or more limbs missing.[1] For these men, returning home did not always mean they were able to perform the same work they had done before the war.

Most Union soldiers received a lump sum final payment of $250 for their service (approximately about $3,700 today).[2] In addition, they could qualify for a generous pension from the US government. Confederate soldiers, however, received no payment from the government, nor did they qualify for pensions. Volunteer organizations attempted to outfit injured soldiers with artificial limbs, but state governments were not able to offer pensions or housing until after Reconstruction had ended.

BROTHER AGAINST BROTHER

Unlike most wars, which pit one country against another, the American Civil War produced many instances of brother fighting against brother. Many families—like the nation—were divided on both sides of the issues.

Franklin Buchanan, captain of the Confederate ship CSS *Virginia*, met his brother in battle during his first engagement. He was wounded in battle, but his brother, McKean Buchanan, was killed. Brothers James and William Terrill both rose to the rank of brigadier general, one for the Union, and the other for the Confederacy. They both died in combat.

POSTWAR NORTH AND SOUTH

Northerners returned to busy cities with industry and job prospects. The North had been affected far less by the devastation of war than the South had been. Factories and industry continued to produce goods and provide plentiful employment, and transportation and businesses were still thriving.

Many Confederate veterans, however, returned to towns and cities that had been destroyed and farm fields that were ruined. With no money, no opportunities

Across the South, thousands of buildings had been destroyed. Many of those buildings, such as the Richmond Railroad Depot, could not be repaired. They had to be completely rebuilt.

for employment, and sometimes no homes, the outlook for many ex-Confederate soldiers was bleak. The South's economic and social structures were destroyed.

Many Northerners favored Reconstruction because they believed the North ought to help the South rebuild. In addition, there were ample business opportunities in the South. Northerners with money to invest could buy cheap land. Factories were needed to produce materials for construction, and railroad building was a thriving necessity.

THE EMOTIONAL TOLL OF WAR

In addition to physical wounds and scars, veterans felt the emotional effect the war had left on them. Thousands ended up in institutions, experiencing what today's medical professionals would diagnose as post-traumatic stress disorder, or PTSD. These former soldiers suffered from paranoia, apathy, listlessness, night terrors, hallucinations, and other symptoms.

The medical records of one Civil War veteran in the Indiana Hospital for the Insane explained he "Sobbed & cried & imagined that some one was going to kill him."[3] Records indicate that some veterans survived the long, bloody war only to return home and commit suicide.

THE LOST

Approximately one in every four Civil War soldiers died.[4] When the war began, the armies were woefully ill prepared to handle the amount of death that occurred. The United States had no national cemeteries. There were no messengers to report news

DISABILITY PENSIONS

On July 14, 1862, President Lincoln approved a pension act that offered benefits to soldiers who sustained injuries or disease during the war resulting in a disability. The secretary of the interior, J. P. Upshur, praised Lincoln's foresight, calling it, "the wisest and most [generous] enactment of the kind ever adapted by any nation."[5]

In 1864, special benefits were created for disabilities resulting in severe impairment, such as:

- $25 per month for loss of both eyes or both hands
- $20 for the loss of both feet
- $20 for the loss of one hand and one foot[6]

of loss to families. The United States had no provisions for identifying the bodies of the dead or giving them a proper burial. By April 1865, tens of thousands of fallen soldiers lay on battlefields, unburied and unidentified. Many more had been quickly buried, often in mass graves with other dead soldiers.

Countless families never learned what had happened to their sons, husbands, fathers, and brothers. They simply knew these men never returned home. The inability to lay these men to rest with proper burials was heart wrenching for loved ones. Soldiers who survived gruesome battles were often forced to leave hundreds of dead fellow soldiers on the ground and move on.

In February 1867, Congress passed legislation to create and protect national cemeteries. Four million dollars of funding was allocated to re-inter the bodies of Union soldiers in 74 national cemeteries. All recovered African-American soldiers were buried in separate areas of the national cemeteries.

The US government made no plans to bury fallen Confederate soldiers. White Southerners reclaimed and buried hundreds of thousands of their dead soldiers themselves. They felt great anger and grief that the government had abandoned their dead loved ones. The resentment would last for years to come.

GRAND ARMY OF THE REPUBLIC

As time passed, veterans realized that those of them who had lived, fought, foraged and survived together had developed a unique bond that could not be broken. There was a sense of loneliness after leaving their regiments and returning to civilian life. Strong friendships formed in battle, and veterans longed for the companionship of their comrades. Organizations began to form to help connect these veterans. At first, they simply served to offer veterans camaraderie, but eventually they provided veterans with unified political power as well.

The most extensive of these organizations was the Grand Army of the Republic (GAR), which was founded on April 6, 1866. Former Union surgeon Benjamin Franklin Stephenson created the GAR in Decatur, Illinois, to serve as

REMEMBERING THE FALLEN

The Grand Army of the Republic (GAR) was an organization of Civil War veterans. Members attended meetings and provided funds for needy veterans and their families. GAR members also sought to honor those who had died in the war.

On May 5, 1878, GAR's leader, General John Logan, issued General Orders No. 11. It designated May 30, 1868, as a day for "strewing with flowers or otherwise decorating the graves of comrades who died in defense of their country during the late rebellion."[7]

This event was first called Decoration Day, but today it is known as Memorial Day. It became a national holiday in 1971, and it is observed on the last Monday in May. On this day, many Americans pin poppy flowers to their shirts. It is a visible way to honor the nation's fallen soldiers and remember their sacrifices.

a platform for former Union soldiers to share their experiences. In the 1890s, membership totaled more than 400,000, and the GAR had significant political influence.[8] It fought for pensions and proper care for its members.

Former Confederate soldiers also established a veterans' organization. The United Confederate Veterans (UCV) created relief associations that provided for war widows and orphans. The UCV also worked to secure pensions for its members from state governments. By the early 1900s, there were more than 160,000 members.[9]

This 1884 poster depicts the GAR's three cardinal principles: Fraternity, Charity, and Loyalty.

WITNESS TO WAR
THE IMPACT OF PHOTOGRAPHS

In the mid-1800s, photography was a medium and art form that was just coming of age, only having been invented in 1839. While it had its limitations, such as only being able to capture subjects that were still, photography was revolutionary. For the first time in history, authentic images could be preserved indefinitely.

More than 5,000 photographers recorded the Civil War as it happened.[10] The best known of these photographers is Mathew Brady. He organized a group of photographers to follow the troops. They carried their heavy, bulky equipment and developing chemicals across the country in horse-drawn wagons. The backs of the wagons served as their darkrooms.

Brady and his photographers took more than 10,000 pictures of the Civil War.[11] They captured battlefields, camps, towns, and people who had experienced the war. Americans saw images of the death and gore from the battlefields. They saw the suffering and ruin in the rubble heaps across the South.

The photographs impacted the way Americans viewed the war. Images of dead soldiers were jarring for Americans, many of whom had never been on a battlefield. The images of the destruction in the South also demonstrate the massive undertaking of Reconstruction.

Andrew Russell, a photographer working with Mathew Brady, took this image of Richmond, Virginia. It lay in ruin after 6,000 Union cavalry overran the city and set fire to more than 800 buildings in April 1865.

A political cartoon mocks carpetbagger Carl Schurz. He moved from Wisconsin to Missouri, where he was elected to the US Senate as a Republican.

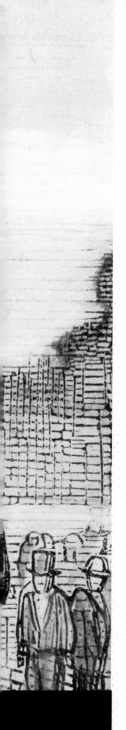

POSTWAR PROGRESS AND STRUGGLES

Thousands of Northerners moved to the South following the war. Teachers wanted to educate freed slaves. Business leaders hoped to start new companies. Politicians sought power in the newly created state governments. The *Daily Mail* of Montgomery, Alabama, coined the term *carpetbaggers* for these Northerners.

The name referred to the luggage some Northerners used when they moved to the South. Their inexpensive bags were made of heavy, secondhand carpet. Southerners viewed these Northerners with contempt. One historian of the era called them "too depraved, dissolute, dishonest, and degraded to get the lowest of places in the states they had just left."[1]

CARPETBAGGERS

The article in Montgomery's *Daily Mail* that coined the term *carpetbaggers* was about Charles A. Miller. Miller was a delegate to the Alabama Convention, the organization that created a new state constitution. The newspaper tried to research his background, but journalists could not find anyone who knew him. People grew skeptical about his motives. They believed he wanted to gain political power and impose Northern values.

Unlike Miller, some carpetbaggers were seen as honorable, qualified leaders. One was Albion Tourgée. He was a former Union solider and judge from Massachusetts. Tourgée moved to Greensboro, North Carolina, in 1865. In his role as a judge, he fought for equal rights. Tourgée also founded schools for African Americans and encouraged the development of railways. Tourgée grew to become one of Greensboro's leading citizens.

NEW GOVERNMENTS AT WORK

Northern and Southern whites and African Americans coexisted in the South, but not without difficulty. There were disagreements over what roles, if any, African Americans should play in the new state governments. Further tensions surrounded the idea of enfranchising former slaves and the question of whether ex-Confederates should be allowed to vote or hold public office.

As state governments were reestablished, state legislatures were filled with Republicans due to the large number of new African-American voters. They worked to abolish the Black Codes and set up schools, hospitals, orphanages, and prisons. They enacted new laws to help sharecroppers and protect workers' rights. Some states passed laws that required white fathers to provide financial support to any children they had

An 1872 portrait of the first African Americans elected to the US Congress (*left to right*): Hiram R. Revels (MS), Benjamin S. Turner (AL), Robert Carlos De Large (SC), Josiah T. Walls (FL), Jefferson F. Long (GA), Joseph H. Rainey (SC), and Robert B. Elliot (SC)

with African-American mothers. Other states, such as South Carolina, provided medical care for the poor.

BLACK RECONSTRUCTION

For the first time in history, African Americans began taking leadership roles in government. At the beginning of Reconstruction, whites assumed prominent roles in government. Soon, however, African Americans were elected to the US Congress. Another 600 won seats in state legislatures, and several others held positions in local government. Thirty-four African Americans became sheriffs in Louisiana and Mississippi.[2]

THE COST OF RECONSTRUCTION

To build schools, shops, churches, railroads, harbors and all the other buildings and components of Southern infrastructure required an immense amount of money. Southern taxes were raised to pay for the spending. In South Carolina, property taxes doubled from their prewar levels.[3]

State debts mushroomed. South Carolina's debt jumped from $5 million in 1868 to more than $16 million three years later.[4] Some legislators made matters worse by engaging in corruption and extravagance. In 1871, South Carolina's legislators gave themselves high salaries and even granted a bonus to the Speaker of the House to help him clear up some gambling debts.

ANIMOSITY & VIOLENCE

As freed slaves made progress in areas such as education and politics, hatred on the part of some white Southerners grew. They formed secret societies in parts of the South. Their mission was to use terror and scare tactics to overturn reforms set in place by Reconstruction.

The most notable terrorist group was the Ku Klux Klan. The Klan began as a social club around 1865. It was started by a group of former Confederate soldiers in Tennessee. Within two years, it had spread across the South. Klan members came from a variety of backgrounds. Poor farmers, local law enforcement officers, and even some governors backed the Ku Klux Klan.

As scholar and author Eric Foner explains, "In effect, the Klan was a military force serving the interests of the Democratic party, the planter class, and all those who desired the restoration of white supremacy. . . . It aimed to destroy the Republican Party's infrastructure . . . and restore racial subordination to every aspect of Southern life."[5]

Members wore disguises to intimidate their victims and to prevent themselves from being identified. They instilled fear in African Americans throughout the South by burning the homes and property of African Americans or capturing them and beating, whipping, or murdering them during nighttime

SCALAWAGS

Southern whites who supported Reconstruction and Republican ideas were called "scalawags." Many Southerners considered scalawags as traitors who were even more despicable than carpetbaggers. One of the best-known scalawags was Samuel F. Phillips. Phillips grew up in North Carolina and worked as a lawyer and politician. He secured the right for African Americans to testify in trials. In his work as solicitor general, Phillips upheld the convictions of Ku Klux Klan members. He is best known for his work in the *Plessy v. Ferguson* case, in which he argued against the separate-but-equal policies that legalized segregation in the South.

raids. They also prevented many from voting, either physically or by using threats of violence.

Anyone who voted Republican, regardless of skin color, risked eviction, violence, or death at the hands of Klan members. Klan members murdered Congressman James M. Hinds of Arkansas, along with three South Carolina state legislators. In Louisiana, approximately 200 African Americans were murdered in one parish, or county, alone.[6]

Combating the Ku Klux Klan's violence proved difficult. Witnesses were too fearful to come forward and testify, and white juries seldom found another white

This illustration shows Klan members from Mississippi wearing their disguises when they were captured in 1872.

person guilty of crimes against African Americans. Some governors in the South utilized militias to arrest Klan members. In Texas, Governor Edmund Davis's militia arrested 6,000 men suspected to be Klansmen.[7] Some counties and states were able to end Klan violence, but the violence continued in other areas of the South.

Congress had to address the ongoing crimes against African Americans and some whites by the Ku Klux Klan. On May 31, 1870, Congress passed the first of three Enforcement Acts. It imposed fines and imprisonment on anyone preventing a registered voter from casting his ballot through physical violence, threats of bodily harm, or any other means.

Another Enforcement Act, known as the Ku Klux Klan Act, made it a federal crime to conspire to prevent a citizen from voting or serving in office or on a jury. It also allowed the president to use military force if needed. This act was successful in bringing about a degree of peace throughout the South after nearly 600 people were charged and convicted.[8]

"Of the slain there were enough to furnish forth a battlefield, and all from those three classes—the negro, the scalawag, and the carpet bagger—all killed with deliberation, overwhelmed by numbers, roused from slumber at the murk midnight, in the hall for public assembly, upon the river brink, on the lonely woods road, in simulation of the public execution—shot, stabbed, hanged, drowned, mutilated beyond description, tortured beyond conception."[9]

—Albion Tourgée, Union soldier and Radical Republican

President Grant signed the Ku Klux Klan Act into law on April 20, 1871. It expanded the federal government's power to protect voters.

Although Klan violence diminished over time, racial conflict continued in the South. The Klan had struck fear in many, and African Americans would fear the group for years to come.

HIRAM RHODES REVELS

1827–1901

Hiram Rhodes Revels was born free in North Carolina in 1827. His father was a Baptist preacher, and his mother was part Scottish. Revels learned to read and write while attending a free school for African-American children. He then went on to work for a short time as a barber.

In 1844, he moved north to attend the Beech Grove Quaker Seminary in Liberty, Indiana. He went on to the Darke County Seminary for African-American students in Ohio. He became an ordained minister of the African Methodist Episcopal Church. During the Civil War, he served as an army chaplain.

In 1870, Revels was selected to fill Mississippi's vacant seat in the US Senate, which had belonged to Jefferson Davis prior to the war. He became the first African American to serve in Congress. He became famous for his well-crafted speeches and his diplomatic approach to politics.

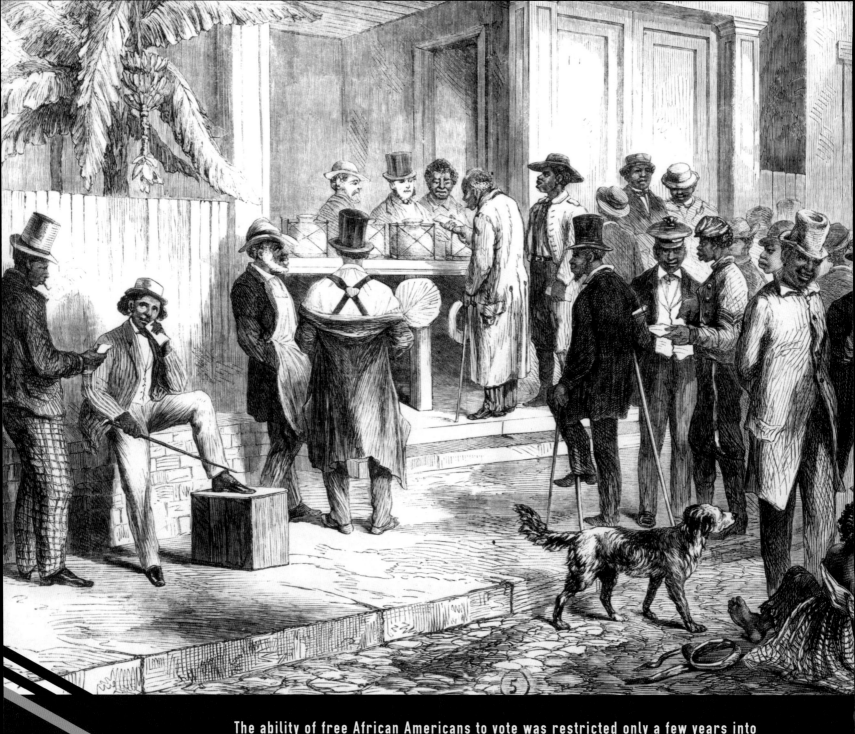

The ability of free African Americans to vote was restricted only a few years into the Reconstruction process.

CHAPTER
★ 8 ★

RECONSTRUCTION ENDS

By 1870, all former Confederate states had fulfilled the requirements of Johnson's Reconstruction plan and had been readmitted to the Union. Up until that time, Republicans had held onto control of most aspects of state and federal government. In the South, the party started losing control of state governments. Southern Democrats blamed the Republican Party for the Civil War and Reconstruction. The threat of Klan violence scared many Southern white Republicans into voting for Democrats and prevented African Americans from voting at all.

By 1874, the Democratic Party successfully regained control of the House of Representatives. Democrats were staunch opponents of the Republican Reconstruction, and therefore the efforts began slowing down.

Federal support for Reconstruction dwindled as its strongest advocates started to pass away. Thaddeus Stevens died in August 1868. Other outspoken radicals, such as Edwin Stanton, Henry Wilson, and Charles Sumner also passed away. President Grant, although effective in bringing many members of the Ku Klux Klan to justice, had lost political support to continue Reconstruction.

In 1875, fighting broke out in Mississippi when a group of whites began attacking Republican political rallies. Governor Adelbert Ames, a Republican, asked President Grant for troops to stop the rioters. South Carolina Republican governor Daniel H. Chamberlain made the same request when six African Americans were shot and killed by white men in the town of Hamburg.[1] Although Grant officially had promised that he would offer aid to uphold civil rights for all, he sent no help.

DEPRESSION HITS THE NORTH

Immediately following the war, railroad construction boomed in the United States. From 1866 to 1873, approximately 35,000 miles (56,000 km) of track were laid, stretching from coast to coast.[2] The railroads employed the largest number of nonagricultural workers in the country.

When Jay Cooke and Company, a large and powerful firm, discovered it had invested too much money in railroad construction and had overextended itself, it declared bankruptcy. This caused a domino effect, leading other businesses and

Postwar railroad construction resulted in many new lines of track throughout the country, but it also led to an economic downturn.

banks that had invested in the railroad to also declare bankruptcy. In two years' time, 18,000 businesses failed. The unemployment rate soared to 14 percent by 1876, and the Northern economy slumped into a depression.[3] Things worsened when, in 1877, railroad workers went on strike, citing wage cuts and poor working conditions. Facing economic woes of their own, Northerners became less interested with the problems in the South.

A NEW LEADER

After an extremely close presidential election against Democrat Samuel J. Tilden, Republican Rutherford B. Hayes became president on March 4, 1877. He officially ended Reconstruction when he removed the last troops from South Carolina, Florida, and Louisiana. These were the only remaining states with Republican leaders, and the troops had been used to protect them from violence. With the troops gone, 12 years of Reconstruction came to a close.

With Republicans gone, Democrats could manipulate elections. They wanted to be able to control who got new positions. If it looked likely a candidate Democrats did not like would win a local election, legislatures would change the position to make it an appointed one instead of an elected one. Legislators could then appoint whomever they chose to fill it. Often the people appointed were powerful and wealthy white men. Gradually, African Americans lost the freedoms Reconstruction had created.

WHAT YOU GIVE TO ONE CLASS YOU MUST GIVE TO ALL.

WHAT YOU DENY TO ONE CLASS YOU SHALL DENY TO ALL.

HON. R. B. ELLIOTT'S speach page 4.

South Carolina representative Robert B. Elliot spoke in favor of the Civil Rights Act.

Sharecroppers often needed all family members to help with planting and harvesting. Jewel Walker, age 6, helped her family by picking cotton in Oklahoma.

THE LEGACY OF RECONSTRUCTION

During Reconstruction, the approximately 4 million freed slaves experienced a series of victories and losses. They had won the right to vote, only to lose it by force or intimidation. They had left the cruelty of the slave owner's whip, only to face the violence of the Ku Klux Klan. Although slavery had ended, the quest for equality remained.

One of the legacies of Reconstruction is the sharecropping system. After the war, the South's economy had been terribly weakened. Cash was scarce, and plantation owners did not have money to hire field hands. Freed slaves lacked the money to buy their own farmland and supplies. This set of circumstances

created a system known as sharecropping. It lasted for several decades
after Reconstruction.

Sharecroppers rented land from plantation owners. Instead of being paid wages, sharecroppers received a share of the crop once it was harvested. Because of this, sharecroppers had to pay for farm supplies, food, clothing, and rent on credit. After the harvest was complete, sharecroppers had to pay for these items. But often, the profits they received were not enough to clear the debt. Many sharecroppers remained poor and landless.

"After freedom, we worked on shares a while. . . . When we worked on shares, we couldn't make nothing, just overalls and something to eat. Half went to the other man and you would destroy your half if you weren't careful. A man that didn't know how to count would always lose. . . . You could get anything you wanted as long as you worked. If you didn't make no money, that's all right; they would advance you more. But you better not leave him, you better not try to leave and get caught. They'd keep you in debt."[1]

—Henry Blake,
African-American sharecropper

JIM CROW LAWS

Jim Crow laws were another legacy of Reconstruction. Southern governments began passing these laws in the 1890s. They ushered in segregation, which prohibited African Americans from using the same facilities as whites. African Americans were no longer allowed in the same schools, parks, libraries, restaurants, railroad cars, or other public places as

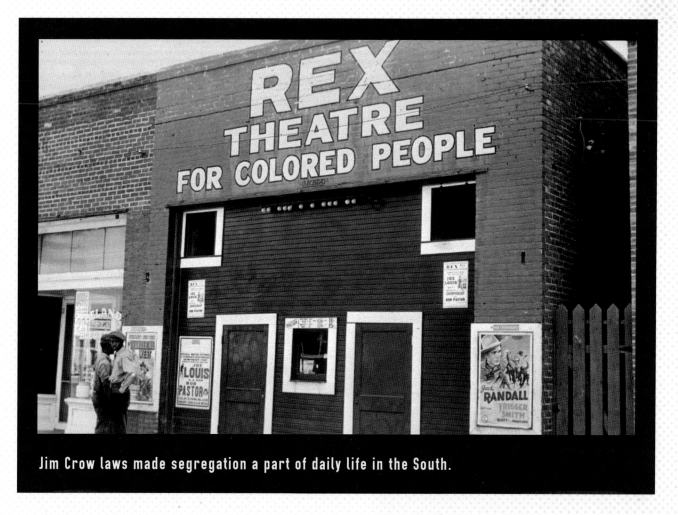

Jim Crow laws made segregation a part of daily life in the South.

whites. There were separate facilities designated for "Colored" people, but these were nearly always inferior to the ones reserved for "Whites Only."

Determining who was considered African American was complex. The South adopted the "one drop rule." It meant that even if a person had only one drop of "black blood," they were considered "negro," the term used at the time to describe African Americans. They were then subjected to racism and segregation.

Segregation laws took away many of the rights Reconstruction had delivered to newly freed slaves. African Americans across the South protested, but the federal government was no longer willing to help. Local governments upheld the Jim Crow laws, and vigilantes used acts of intimidation and violence to ensure African Americans complied.

Jim Crow laws lasted for decades. Then on May 17, 1954, the US Supreme Court declared laws that required separate public schools for whites and African Americans were unconstitutional. The lawsuit developed when Oliver L. Brown sued the school board of Topeka, Kansas. Brown's third grade daughter, Linda, was forced to walk several blocks to catch a bus that would drive her miles farther to reach the

LIVING UNDER JIM CROW

Some examples of Jim Crow laws that were enacted in the South included:

- "No person or corporation shall require any white female nurse to nurse in wards or rooms in hospitals, either public or private, in which negro men are placed." (Alabama)
- "It shall be unlawful for a negro and white person to play together or in company with each other at any game of pool or billiards." (Alabama)
- "No colored barber shall serve as a barber [to] white women or girls." (Georgia)
- "Books shall not be interchangeable between the white and colored schools, but shall continue to be used by the race first using them." (North Carolina)[2]

Integrated schools became more common after the US Supreme Court ruled against segregated schools in 1954.

President Lyndon B. Johnson speaks to the nation on television before signing the Civil Rights Act of 1964.

TWENTIETH-CENTURY RECONSTRUCTION

While fighting for civil rights in 1967, Dr. Martin Luther King Jr. suggested that perhaps the United States needed another dose of reconstruction:

> The black revolution is much more than a struggle for the rights of Negroes. It is, rather, forcing America to face all its interrelated flaws: racism, poverty, militarism, and materialism. It is exposing evils that are rooted deeply in the whole structure of our society. It reveals systematic rather than superficial flaws, and it suggests that radical reconstruction of society itself is the real issue to be faced.[3]

black school. The white school, however, was only blocks away, and far superior to the school she was forced to attend.

THE LONG JOURNEY TO FREEDOM

In the 1950s and 1960s, African-American leaders strove to put an end to the racism and segregation they and their ancestors had endured for more than 300 years. Inspirational leaders such as Dr. Martin Luther King Jr., Malcolm X, and Rosa Parks helped lead the civil rights movement in the 1950s.

The tenacious work, dedication, and bravery of many African Americans led to progress. On July 2, 1964, President Lyndon B. Johnson signed the Civil Rights Act of 1964. It required schools and public facilities to be integrated. The law also banned employers from discriminating against people based on race, color, religion, sex, or national origin.

A CHANGING PERSPECTIVE

Before the Civil War, many Americans considered themselves citizens of their state first and foremost. The war changed that. In the North, many people viewed themselves as belonging to a unified nation. They began saying "the United States is" rather than "the United States are." In the South, however, animosity and resentment toward Northerners lingered for decades. The states' rights to make political decisions for themselves has been debated since the Civil War.

Reconstruction and the decades that followed it brought about landmark changes for the United States. Three amendments to the US Constitution promised great changes for freed people. Many of these changes are part of daily life now. However, racism and violence are still a reality for many African Americans today. The leaders who carry out the legacy of Lincoln, Sumner, and Stevens still have much work to do.

Today's activists, including those in the Black Lives Matter movement, continue to

TIMELINE

April 12, 1861
Confederate troops fire on US military post Fort Sumter in Charleston Harbor, South Carolina, beginning the Civil War.

September 22, 1862
Abraham Lincoln demands all seceded states return to the Union.

January 1, 1863
Lincoln issues the Emancipation Proclamation, freeing slaves in the rebellious Southern states.

December 8, 1863
Lincoln issues the Proclamation of Amnesty and Reconstruction, marking the start of Reconstruction.

May 29, 1865
President Andrew Johnson grants pardons to many high-ranking Confederate officers.

April 9, 1866
Congress passes the Civil Rights Act, which guarantees citizenship to all people born in the United States.

March 2, 1867
Congress passes the first Reconstruction Act.

July 9, 1868
The Fourteenth Amendment grants full citizenship to all people born or naturalized in the United States.

November 8, 1864

President Lincoln is reelected to a second term.

January 31, 1865

The Thirteenth Amendment ends slavery.

April 9,1865

The Civil War ends when General Lee surrenders at Appomattox Courthouse in Virginia.

April 14, 1865

John Wilkes Booth assassinates President Lincoln in Ford's Theatre in Washington, DC.

February 3, 1870

The Fifteenth Amendment prohibits disenfranchisement based on race, color, or previous condition of servitude.

March 4, 1877

Rutherford B. Hayes becomes president, and Reconstruction ends shortly after he is inaugurated.

May 17, 1954

The US Supreme Court declares segregation unconstitutional.

July 2, 1964

President Lyndon B. Johnson signs the Civil Rights Act of 1964, which requires public facilities to be integrated.

ESSENTIAL FACTS

KEY PLAYERS

- Abraham Lincoln was the president who led the Union against the Confederacy in the American Civil War.

- Andrew Johnson was the president who oversaw Reconstruction after the American Civil War and was later impeached.

- Thaddeus Stevens was a Radical Republican, member of the US House of Representatives, and leader in the impeachment trial against President Johnson.

KEY PRESIDENTIAL AND CONGRESSIONAL ACTIONS

- Emancipation Proclamation issued, 1863: President Lincoln's declaration freed 4 million slaves in the Confederate states.

- Thirteenth Amendment ratified, 1865: This amendment to the US Constitution formally abolished slavery throughout the United States.

- Civil Rights Act of 1866: The act granted citizenship and equal rights to African-American men in the United States.

- Reconstruction Acts, 1867: These acts reorganized former Confederate states and established plans to readmit them to the Union.

- Tenure of Office Act, 1867: This act prevented the president from removing officeholders without the approval of the Senate.

- Fourteenth Amendment, 1868: This amendment granted citizenship to all persons born or naturalized in the United States.

- Fifteenth Amendment, 1870: This amendment granted African-American men the right to vote.

- Civil Rights Act of 1875: This federal law was enacted to guarantee African Americans had equal access to public accommodations.

IMPACT ON SOCIETY

Reconstruction was the process by which the former Confederate states were rebuilt and readmitted to the Union. It resulted in the abolition of slavery and new state governments in the South. Reconstruction created resentment in the South. Ultimately, it forever changed the lives of freed slaves but, due to animosity in the South, also helped spawn hate groups such as the Ku Klux Klan.

QUOTE

"After freedom, we worked on shares a while. . . . When we worked on shares, we couldn't make nothing, just overalls and something to eat. Half went to the other man and you would destroy your half if you weren't careful. A man that didn't know how to count would always lose. . . . You could get anything you wanted as long as you worked. If you didn't make no money, that's all right; they would advance you more. But you better not leave him, you better not try to leave and get caught. They'd keep you in debt."

—Henry Blake, African-American sharecropper

GLOSSARY

ABOLITIONIST
A person who wants to end slavery.

AMNESTY
An official pardon granted to people who have been convicted of political offenses or crimes.

ELECTORAL VOTE
A vote cast by a member of the Electoral College, the collection of people who elect the president of the United States.

EMANCIPATION
The act of freeing an individual or group from slavery.

FREEDMEN
People who have been freed from slavery.

IMPEACH
To charge an elected official with wrongdoing.

MANIFESTO
A public declaration of opinion.

PENSION
A regular payment made to a retired person as a reward for past services, or to help someone suffering from an injury or other need.

RATIFY
To formally approve or adopt an idea or document.

SECESSION
The formal withdrawal of one group or region from a political union.

SEGREGATION
The practice of separating groups of people based on race, gender, ethnicity, or other factors.

SOVEREIGN
Possessing ultimate power.

VAGRANCY
The act of wandering from place to place, often asking for money.

VIGILANTE
A person who attempts to enforce the law in a community but has no legal authority to do so.

WHITE SUPREMACY
The belief that white people are superior to all other races.

ADDITIONAL RESOURCES

SELECTED BIBLIOGRAPHY

Du Bois, W. E. B. *Black Reconstruction in America.* New York: Oxford UP, 2007. Print.

Foner, Eric. *Reconstruction: America's Unfinished Revolution, 1863-1877.* New York: Perennial Classics, 2002. Print.

Robertson, James. *After the Civil War: The Heroes, Villains, Soldiers, and Civilians Who Changed America.* Washington, DC: National Geographic, 2015. Print.

FURTHER READINGS

Cocca, Lisa Colozza. *Reconstruction and the Aftermath of the Civil War.* New York: Crabtree, 2012. Print.

Osborne, Linda Barrett. *Traveling the Freedom Road: From Slavery & the Civil War through Reconstruction.* New York: Abrams, 2009. Print.

WEBSITES

To learn more about Essential Library of the Civil War, visit **booklinks.abdopublishing.com**. These links are routinely monitored and updated to provide the most current information available.

PLACES TO VISIT

National Civil Rights Museum
450 Mulberry Street
Memphis, TN 38103
901-521-9699
http://civilrightsmuseum.org
Located at the site where Dr. Martin Luther King Jr. was assassinated, the museum has several permanent exhibits focusing on the civil rights movement of the 1900s. It also has a number of exhibits detailing the Atlantic slave trade, the wealth that slaveholding produced, the end of slavery, and the rise of Jim Crow segregation.

Nicodemus National Historic Site
304 Washington Avenue
Nicodemus, KS 67625
785-839-4233
http://www.nps.gov/nico/index.htm
Walk the streets of Nicodemus, Kansas. It is the oldest and only remaining settlement west of the Mississippi River that freed slaves built during the Reconstruction era.

SOURCE NOTES

CHAPTER 1. THE FALL OF ATLANTA

1. Marc Wortman. "Atlanta's Fall Foretold the End of Civil War Bloodshed." *Daily Beast*. Daily Beast, 1 Sept. 2014. Web. 5 Feb. 2016.

2. Geoffrey C. Ward. *The Civil War: An Illustrated History*. New York: Knopf, 1990. Print. 340.

3. Ibid. 344.

4. Michael Rose. *Atlanta: A Portrait of the Civil War*. Charleston, SC: Arcadia, 1999. Print. 9.

5. Margaret E. Wagner, et al. eds. *The Library of Congress Civil War Desk Reference*. New York: Simon, 2002. Print. 45.

6. "Civil War Battles." *HistoryNet*. World History Group, 12 Sept. 2015. Web. 5 Feb. 2016.

7. *The Civil War: A Visual History*. New York: DK, 2015. Print. 293.

8. Margaret E. Wagner, et al. eds. *The Library of Congress Civil War Desk Reference*. New York: Simon, 2002. Print. 733.

CHAPTER 2. WAR

1. Joseph C. G. Kennedy. *Population of the United States in 1860*. Washington, DC: Government Printing Office, 1864. Web. 598–599.

2. David R. Meyer. *The Roots of American Industrialization*. Baltimore, MD: Johns Hopkins UP, 2003. Print. 2.

3. "American Civil War." *Encyclopaedia Britannica*. Encyclopaedia Britannica, 2015. Web. 5 Feb. 2016.

4. "Civil War Casualties." *Civil War Trust*. Civil War Trust, 2014. Web. 5 Feb. 2016.

5. "Maimed Men." *US National Library of Medicine*. National Institutes of Health, 17 Mar. 2011. Web. 5 Feb. 2016.

6. Judith E. Harper. *Women During the Civil War: An Encyclopedia*. New York: Routledge, 2004. Print. 335.

7. Geoffrey C. Ward. *The Civil War: An Illustrated History*. New York: Knopf, 1990. Print. 342.

8. Lisa Tendrich Frank. *Women in the American Civil War, Volume 1*. Santa Barbara, CA: ABC-CLIO, 2008. Web. 206–207.

9. Benjamin T. Arrington. "Industry and Economy during the Civil War." *National Park Service*. National Park Service, n.d. Web. 5 Feb. 2016.

10. "The Story of Confederate Currency." *Virtual Gettysburg*. Another Software Miracle, LLC, 2002. Web. 5 Feb. 2016.

11. Ibid.

CHAPTER 3. LINCOLN'S RECONSTRUCTION

1. "Emancipation Proclamation." *Encyclopaedia Britannica*. Encyclopaedia Britannica, 2015. Web. 5 Feb. 2016.

2. Eric Foner. *Reconstruction: America's Unfinished Revolution*. New York: Harper, 1988. Print. 49.

3. "The Wade-Davis Reconstruction Bill." *History, Art & Archives*. US House of Representatives, n.d. Web. 5 Feb. 2016.

4. "The War upon the President" *New York Times*. New York Times, 9 Aug. 1864. Web. 5 Feb. 2016.

5. "The 13th Amendment." *History, Art & Archives*. US House of Representatives, n.d. Web. 5 Feb. 2016.

6. *US Constitution*. Amendment XIII, Sections 1 and 2.

CHAPTER 4. JOHNSON'S RECONSTRUCTION

1. Christopher J. Olsen. *The American Civil War*. New York: Hill and Wang, 2006. Print. 228–229.

2. Harold Holzer. "What the Newspapers Said When Lincoln Was Killed." *Smithsonian Magazine*. Smithsonian, Mar. 2015. Web. 5 Feb. 2016.

3. Ibid.

4. *The Civil War: A Visual History*. New York: DK, 2015. Print. 338.

5. "Wade-Davis Bill." *Our Documents*. National Archives & Records Administration, n.d. Web. 5 Feb. 2016.

6. "Civil Rights Act of 1866." 14 Stat. 27–30. 9 Apr. 1866.

7. "Blacks Vote for the First Time in the South." *History Engine*. University of Richmond, 2015. Web. 5 Feb. 2016.

8. Robert C. Kennedy. "Andrew Johnson's Reconstruction, and How It Works." *Harp Week*. New York Times, 2001. Web. 5 Feb. 2016.

9. Christopher J. Olsen. *The American Civil War*. New York: Hill and Wang, 2006. Print. 244-245.

CHAPTER 5. RECONSTRUCTION FOR AFRICAN AMERICANS

1. Booker T. Washington. *Up from Slavery: An Autobiography*. New York: Signet, 2010. Print. 30.

2. Laurie F. Maffly-Kipp. "The Church in the Southern Black Community." *Documenting the American South*. University of North Carolina, 2004. Web. 5 Feb. 2016.

3. *The War of the Rebellion*. US War Department, 1880–1901, series 2, vol. 5. Print. 795–97.

4. Elsie Freeman, et al. "The Fight for Equal Rights: A Recruiting Poster for Black Soldiers in the Civil War." *Social Education*. Silver Springs, MD: NCSS Publications, Feb. 1992. Print. 118–120.

5. "The 54th Massachusetts Infantry." *History Channel*. History Channel, 2010. Web. 5 Feb. 2016.

6. Margaret E. Wagner, et al. eds. *The Library of Congress Civil War Desk Reference*. New York: Simon, 2002. Print. 777.

7. Joseph C. G. Kennedy. *Population of the United States in 1860*. Washington, DC: Government Printing Office, 1864. Web. 598–599.

SOURCE NOTES
CONTINUED

8. "Lost Friends. Advertisements from the *Southwestern Christian Advocate*." *Historic New Orleans Collection*. Historic New Orleans Collection, 2015. Web. 29 Nov. 2015.

9. Henry Louis Gates Jr. "The Truth Behind '40 Acres and a Mule.'" *The African Americans: Many Rivers to Cross*. WNET, 2013. Web. 5 Feb. 2016.

10. "The Westward Migration." *In Motion: The African American Migration Experience*. New York Public Library, 2005. Web. 5 Feb. 2016.

11. Ibid.

CHAPTER 6. COMING HOME

1. "Civil War Casualties." *Civil War Trust*. Civil War Trust, 2014. Web. 5 Feb. 2016

2. Margaret E. Wagner, et al. eds. *The Library of Congress Civil War Desk Reference*. New York: Simon, 2002. Print. 745.

3. Tony Horwitz. "Did Civil War Soldiers Have PTSD?" *Smithsonian Magazine*. Smithsonian, Jan. 2015. Web. 5 Feb. 2016.

4. "Civil War Casualties." *Civil War Trust*. Civil War Trust, 2014. Web. 5 Feb. 2016.

5. Margaret E. Wagner, et al. eds. *The Library of Congress Civil War Desk Reference*. New York: Simon, 2002. Print. 745.

6. Ibid.

7. "General Orders No. 11." *Washington Times*. Washington Times, 28 May 2010. Web. 5 Feb. 2016.

8. *The Civil War: A Visual History*. New York: DK, 2015. Print. 348.

9. Steven L. Warren. "United Confederate Veterans (UCV)." *Encyclopedia of Arkansas History & Culture*. Central Arkansas Library System, 2015. Web. 5 Feb. 2016.

10. "Welcome to the Center." *Center for Civil War Photography*. Center for Civil War Photography, 2009. Web. 5 Feb. 2016.

11. "Mathew Brady." *Civil War Trust*. Civil War Trust, 2014. Web. 5 Feb. 2016.

CHAPTER 7. POSTWAR PROGRESS AND STRUGGLES

1. Margaret E. Wagner, et al. eds. *The Library of Congress Civil War Desk Reference.* New York: Simon, 2002. Print. 779.

2. Ibid. 782.

3. Allen C. Guelzo. *Fateful Lightning: A New History of the Civil War & Reconstruction.* New York: Oxford, 2012. Print. 503.

4. Ibid.

5. Eric Foner. *A Short History of Reconstruction.* New York: Harper, 1990. Print. 425–426.

6. Margaret E. Wagner, et al. eds. *The Library of Congress Civil War Desk Reference.* New York: Simon, 2002. Print. 785.

7. Ibid.

8. Ibid. 786.

9. Albion W. Tourgée. *A Fool's Errand.* New York: Fords, Howard & Hulbert, 1880. Web. 246.

CHAPTER 8. RECONSTRUCTION ENDS

1. Allen C. Guelzo. *Fateful Lightning: A New History of the Civil War & Reconstruction.* New York: Oxford, 2012. Print. 506.

2. "Ulysses S. Grant." *The American Experience.* WGBH Educational Foundation, 2002. Web. 5 Feb. 2016.

3. Ibid.

CHAPTER 9. THE LEGACY OF RECONSTRUCTION

1. "Henry Blake." *Born in Slavery: Slave Narratives from the Federal Writers' Project.* Library of Congress, 1936–1938. Web. 5 Feb. 2016.

2. "Jim Crow Laws." *Martin Luther King Jr. National Historic Site.* National Park Service, 2 Feb. 2016. Web. 5 Feb. 2016.

3. "The Living King." *Ebony* 41.3 (1986): 62. Web. 5 Feb. 2016.

INDEX

ABOUT THE AUTHOR

Susan E. Hamen has written more than 20 books on various topics for young readers, including *The Wright Brothers*, *Google*, and *The Quest*. Her book *Clara Barton: Civil War Hero and American Red Cross Founder* made the American Library Association's 2011 Amelia Bloomer Project Book List. Hamen lives in Minnesota with her husband, daughter, and son. When she is not writing or editing, she loves to hike, canoe, read with her kids, and travel to and explore National Parks and Historic Sites with her family.